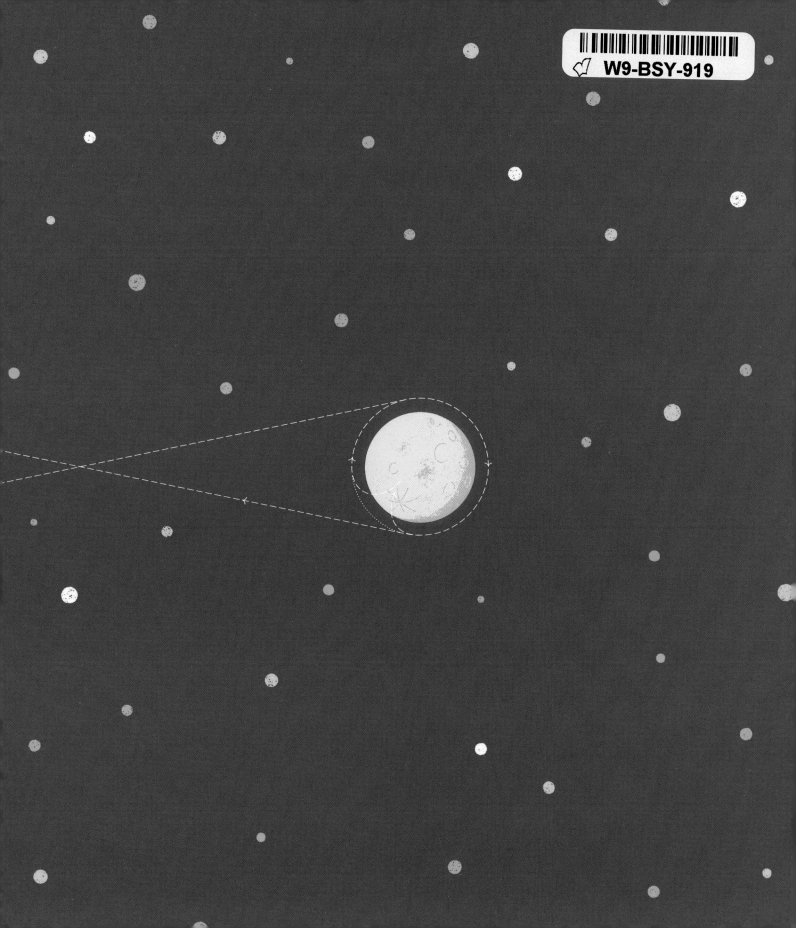

Brimming with creative inspiration, how-to projects, and useful information to enrich your everyday life, Quarto Knows is a favourite destination for those pursuing their interests and passions. Visit our site and dig deeper with our books into your area of interest: Quarto Creates, Quarto Cooks, Quarto Homes, Quarto Lives, Quarto Drives, Quarto Explores, Quarto Gifts, or Quarto Kids.

## IN MEMORY OF MICHAEL COLLINS.

Text © 2021 Zoë Tucker.
Illustrations © 2021 Nick Radford.

First published in 2021 by Wide Eyed Editions, an imprint of The Quarto Group. 100 Cummings Center, Suite 265D, Beverly, MA 01915, USA.
T +1 978-282-9590 F +1 078-283-2742
www.QuartoKnows.com

A CIP record for this book is available from the Library of Congress.

ISBN 978-0-7112-6380-2

The illustrations were created digitally
Set in Lelo
Published by Georgia Amson-Bradshaw
Designed by Zoë Tucker
Production by Dawn Cameron
Manufactured in Guangdong, China, TT072021

9 8 7 6 5 4 3 2 1

FOR SUPERSTAR AVERY -Z.T.

FOR MY OWN LITTLE CREW, HELEN, ERNIE & BRYHER – LOVE YOU TO THE MOON & BACK! X -N.R.

Written by
Zoë Tucker

WE ARE THE

Illustrated by
Nick Radford

# *APOLLO 11 CREW*

EAGLE

WIDE EYED EDITIONS

Mike zipped up his jumpsuit and climbed up into the flight simulator. Today was his first day of training with his crew mates Neil and Buzz. They had six months to get in tip top shape for the biggest and bravest adventure of their life—they were going to the Moon!

FLIGHT
SIMULATOR

No one had ever been to
the Moon before, so training
was hard. They each had a
role to prepare for.

Mike was the pilot of the main spacecraft, called Columbia. It was his job to get them to the Moon, and back home again.

Neil was the cool-as-a-cucumber captain of the mission.

Buzz would fly the Eagle, the tiny spacecraft that would detach from Columbia and take him and Neil down to the Moon's surface.

While Neil and Buzz landed on the Moon, Mike would stay behind on Columbia, orbiting the Moon. He'd be ready to jump in and rescue Neil and Buzz if anything went wrong!

After months of training the big day arrived. The astronauts tumbled out of bed,

had a quick breakfast, and read the newspaper.

They had one final check from the nurse and they were ready to fly!

Neil, Mike, and Buzz put on their space suits and headed to the launch pad. As they waved goodbye to their family and friends they felt nervous, but excited. The eyes of the world were upon them.

BUZZ

MIKE

NEIL

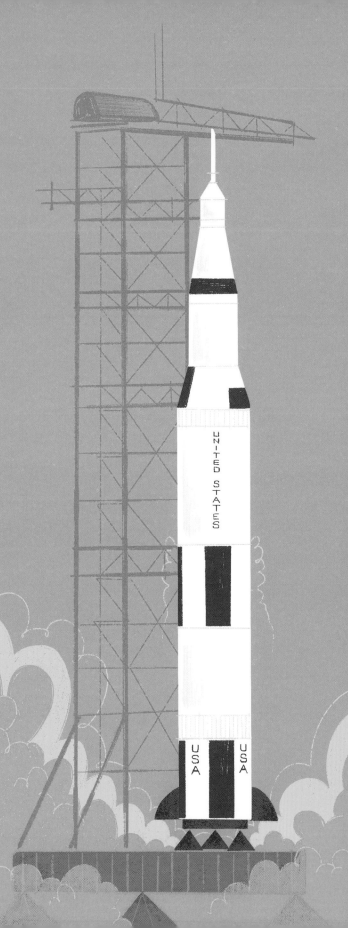

Their spacecraft was perched on top of an enormous rocket. A team of people on the ground called Misson Control were on hand to help them every step of the way.

Finally, it was time for their journey to begin.

They blasted into space!

The rocket swung into orbit around the Earth,
and then zoomed towards the Moon.

Finally, the rocket broke away leaving the
Columbia spacecraft and the lunar module.

Mike then had to move the lunar module round to the front of the spacecraft. It was a very tricky job!

They were traveling super fast. One mistake and the mission would be over. He took a deep breath and got to work.

EAGLE

COLUMBIA

NICE JOB MIKE

LET'S GO TO THE MOON!

The friends took it in turns to move around the cabin to get their jobs done.

Mike and Neil checked all the dials in the flight deck and then reported back to Mission Control,

while Buzz recorded a message for the people back home.

They listened to music,

WHAT GOES UP, MUST COME DOWN!

and ate chicken soup out of special space packets.

They even had butterscotch pudding and warm coffee!

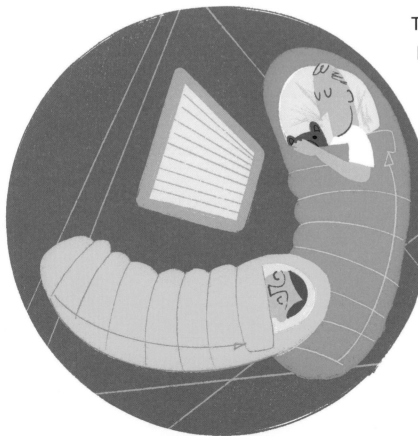

When it was finally time to rest the astronauts covered the windows and drifted off in their sleeping bags.

It took three days to reach the Moon.
Up close it didn't look at all like they imagined.
It was rocky, and covered with enormous craters
and big jagged boulders.

Mike helped Neil and Buzz get ready. They were excited and a little bit scared. It was dangerous and daring and they were going where no human had been before!

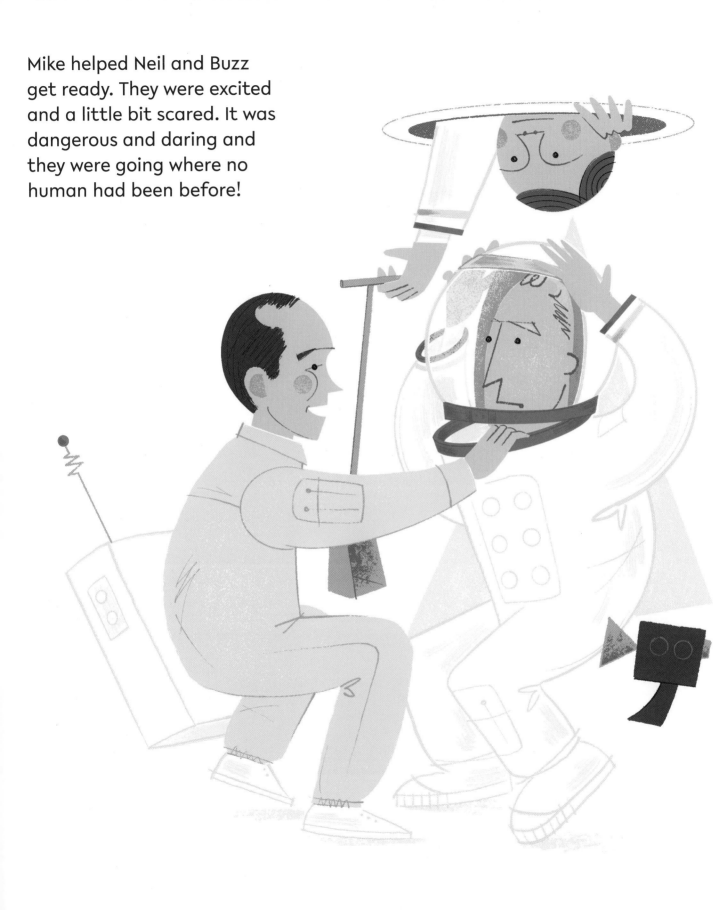

Mike sealed the hatch and the two craft separated.
As the Eagle moved away they said their goodbyes.

Mike watched the Eagle
until it was just a tiny dot
in the distance.

He began his orbit around the
Moon and listened carefully to
Neil and Buzz on the radio as
they began their adventure...

Neil steered the ship, as Buzz watched for danger down below.

LOOK OUT FOR THOSE ROCKS!

AND THE BIG CRATER!

WHOA!

Mike held his breath and listened to
the radio—but suddenly it cut out.
He was all alone.

He searched for his friends
on the Moon's surface, but they
were too far away to see.

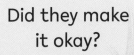

Did they make
it okay?

Suddenly, the radio crackled into life.

MISSION CONTROL, THIS IS NEIL, THE EAGLE HAS LANDED

Neil and Buzz peered out of the window.
It was like nowhere on Earth. They
couldn't wait to step outside!

Neil was first down the ladder.

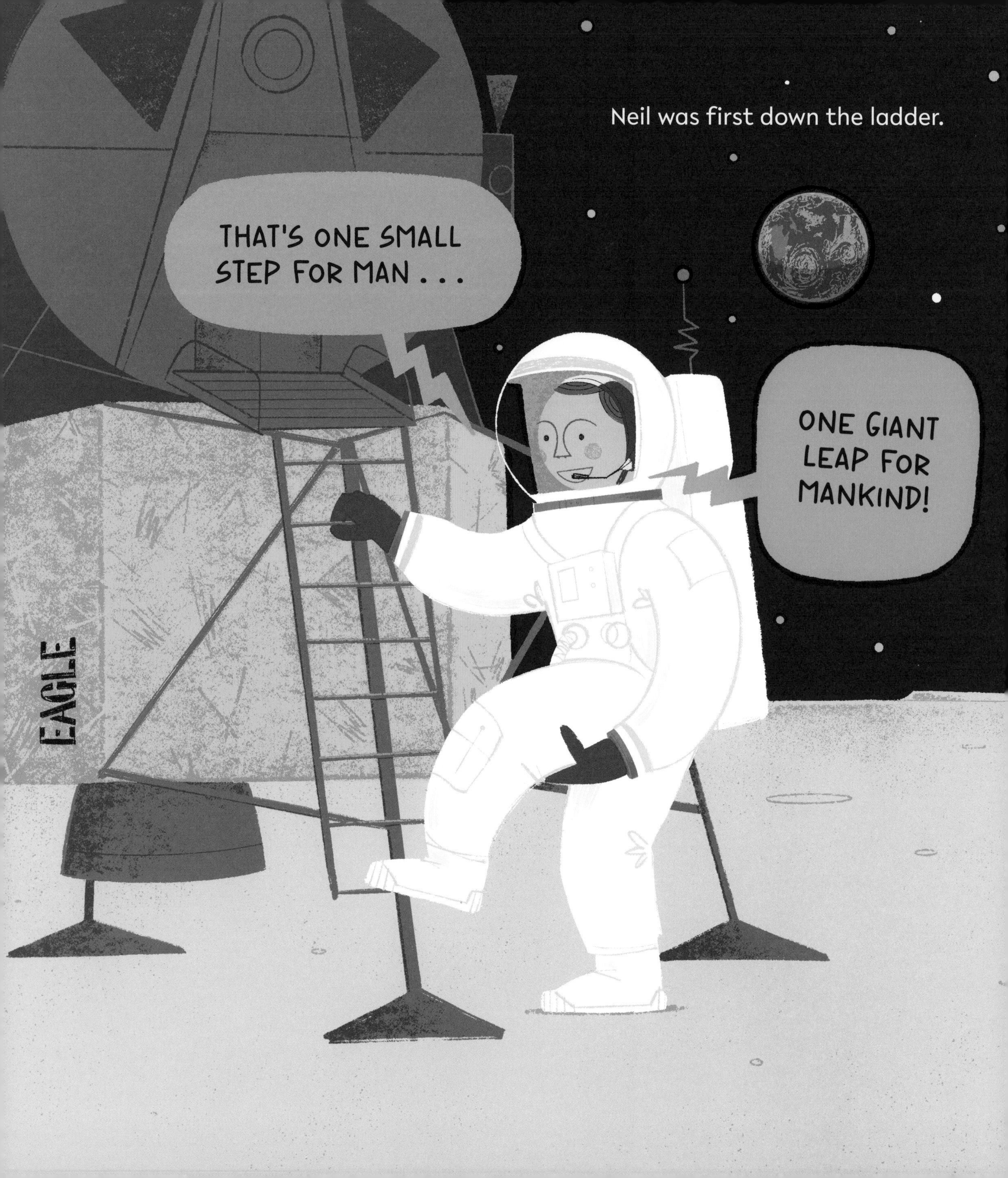

The Moon was covered in a fine layer of dust, and the astronauts left footprints as they bounced along the surface.

First they collected Moon rocks and took photos.

WOW!

Then they sent a message to all the people back at home. They were an inspiration to the whole world.

At last, when it was time to go home, Buzz and Neil climbed back into the Eagle and prepared to take off.

Mike's biggest fear was leaving Neil and Buzz behind. Would they be able to take off from the Moon?

He waited anxiously.

There they were!
Mike watched as the Eagle got closer and closer.

He matched their speed and carefully guided the two spacecraft until they were joined together again.

At last, the crew was back together again.

With one final look out the window, the three astronauts set off for home. Tired and happy, they couldn't wait to get back and tell everyone all about it.

It took three days to get back to Earth. They splashed
down in the ocean and felt the cool sea breeze. They
realised how beautiful and precious our planet is, and
they were happy to be home.

The journey to the Moon was a huge success.
Neil, Buzz, and Mike were brave explorers, daring
to do something that no human had done before.
They worked hard and looked after each other,
and together they reached for the stars!

# WE ARE THE
# ★ APOLLO 11 CREW ★

Neil Armstrong: August 5, 1930—August 25, 2012

Buzz Aldrin: January 20, 1930

Michael Collins: October 31, 1930—28 April 2021

**THE APOLLO 11** crew became the first people to ever set foot on the Moon. Their journey took them far away from their family and friends on Earth, to a place where no one had ever been before. It was exciting and daring, and they needed lots of courage and determination to achieve their dream. Neil Armstrong, Michael Collins, and Buzz Aldrin had six months to train for their adventure. During that time, they lived together as they practiced and rehearsed every step of their planned mission. They knew it was dangerous and risky, and they might not make it back home.

During the 1950s and 1960s, America and the Soviet Union were in a race to become the first country to send people to space. It was called the Space Race! The competition was fierce, and for much of it, the Soviet Union led the way. In 1961 a Russian astronaut called Yuri Gagarin became the first man to orbit Earth, quickly followed by the first woman, Valentina Tereshkova.

The Americans were always a little behind in the race, until July 16, 1969, when the crew of Apollo 11 launched for the Moon.

It took three days to get to the Moon. On the morning of July 20, 1969, Neil and Buzz took the lunar module down to the surface of the Moon, whilst Mike stayed behind in the command module, completely alone.

Mike had a very important role in the mission. As the drama and excitement unfolded below, Mike had to watch and wait. If anything happened to his friends, it was his job to jump in and rescue them. Or worse, travel the long journey home without them. Mike spent almost 24 hours alone, orbiting the Moon 14 times, with intermittent radio contact.

Walking on the Moon was a huge achievement for humankind, and it was only possible because of the hard work of lots of different people. From the brave astronauts who paved the way before them, to the super clever engineers, mathematicians, and scientists who created the spacecraft and the computers to fly them there.

When the astronauts arrived back on Earth they were treated like rock stars and went on a world tour! They met the Queen of England, the King of Norway, and the Emperor of Japan. They even met the pope!

The lunar landing was watched by 600 million people and the crew of Apollo 11 captured the hearts and minds of people not just in America, but all over the world.

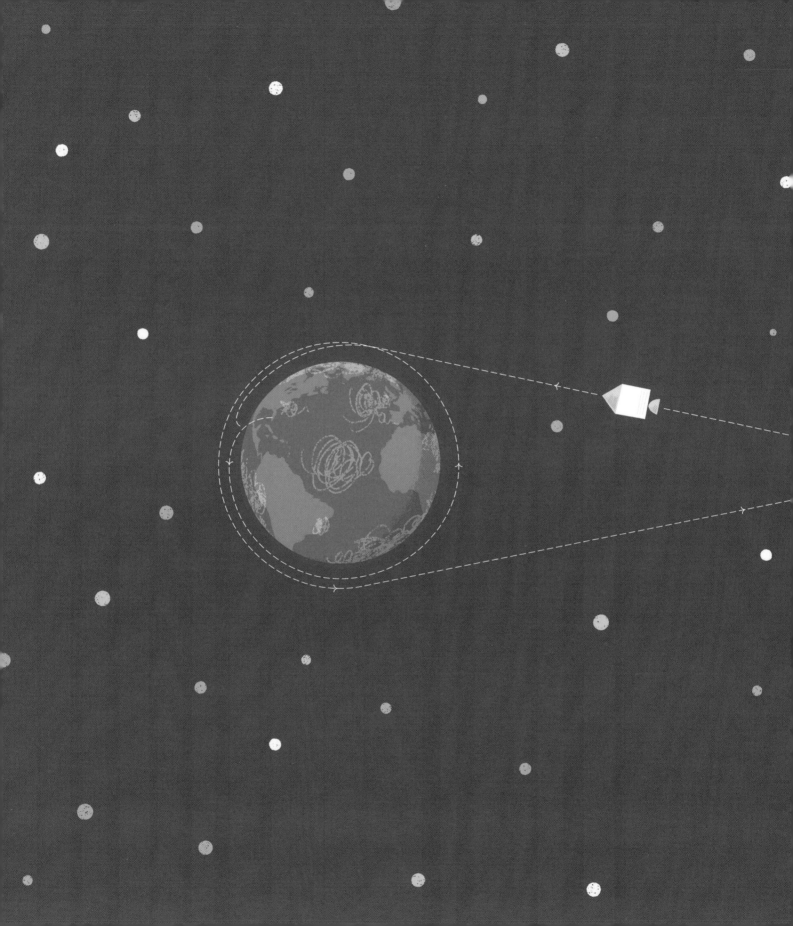